Acknowledgments

We would like to thank all who have helped develop our story, including Gwen, Graham, Luke, Leli, David and Saide, those at the Heart of Life Spirituality Centre (who passionately teach eco-theology), Graeme Galloway and Phil Kreveld (who have been remarkable mentors for Ann in art and life), and the dynamic Christian community at Brunswick Uniting Church.

Key ideas for this book have come from the field of ecotheology, especially from the writings of Pierre Teilhard de Chardin, Thomas Berry, Denis Edwards, Ilia Delio, the Encyclical Letter on Ecology and Climate by Pope Francis (Laudato Si), as well as from indigenous spirituality. Thomas Berry, in particular, mentions the need for a "New Story" for humankind which embraces our underlying scientific understandings as well as traditional beliefs which inform the source and purpose of life. A New Story will guide humanity to really love the "Circle of Love" at the heart of the universe and care for creation.

Richard Arnold, Ann Soo, Thiamhien (Theo) Arnold and Yosef Arnold – November 2021

Introduction

This book is a collaboration between Richard Arnold, a former chemical engineer and retired minister of religion with the Uniting Church in Australia; Anne Soo, a professional social worker who now uses art as tool for healing and empowerment; and two of Richard's grandchildren, Theo (aged 9) and Yosef (aged 7).

The narrative and artwork are aimed at all people, including young people. It evolved out of Richard's interest in reconciling religious faith and science, and his concern for the future wellbeing of our planet. Richard is inspired by eco-theology, which focuses on how faith can inform our relationship with the whole biosphere and how our earthly home, oikos, is related to the Mystery at the heart of creation. Part of this quest also involves embracing two great scientific movements of the last 300 years: the theory of evolution and quantum physics (which includes the nature and origins of energy and matter).

Our story is grounded in the Christian tradition, but also draws on other influences and is ultimately universal in nature. The understanding that informed our story is one that particularly values reason, enquiry, openness to change, and seeks a way of harmony with the whole of creation. We hope that all readers, whether young or old, Christian or not, might identify with the universal images of "Circle of Love" and "stream of love" which are central to our story.

In 2019, Richard and Ann released an initial version of this story which included some amazing artwork from Ann. On a visit to Cambodia in 2020, where Theo and Yosef were accompanying their parents on a diplomatic posting, Richard shared this with his family. In conversation with Theo and Yosef, he became inspired to develop a revised version which might connect with all ages and inspire at all levels of consciousness.

The boys showed rich imagination and came up with some bright and sparky ideas of illustrations to go with the words. Ann loved those ideas so much that she asked if she could draw and paint with the boys over Zoom. So began a beautiful journey every Monday beginning in May 2020, right at the start of the four-month COVID-19 lockdown in Melbourne.

Theo, Yosef, Ann and Richard — with help from the boys' mother, Leli — would get together for an hour of drawing, chatting and being open to the creative spirit flowing through them. Ann watched the boys work and noticed their incredible joy for life and how drawing came so easily and comfortably. COVID-19 brought many worries and concerns into all our lives, but this collaboration was a little oasis that we created for each other — and for you, the reader of this book.

At a time in history when concern for the environment and a just distribution of the Earth's resources is sometimes overshadowed by greed and exploitation, our hope is that our "New Story" might inspire readers to embrace life as a journey within the beautiful creation we call the Universe, and to connect with the stream of love which flowed out from the Circle of Love at the very beginning. As we do this we will grow in love, reverence and respect for our fellow members of the human family and the whole biosphere, through realising that we have all been intimately entwined from the beginning, and will remain so, within a continually evolving universe.

So come and be cradled in the arms of love and experience the incredible journey of the universe !

Before the beginning of time, a community of three danced and joined arms together – they formed a Circle of Love. Then they dreamed that they could share their love and watch it grow.

The three hugged each other so tightly that they created a big bang, causing a stream of love to flow out in all directions.

This stream of love set the whole universe on a journey, filling it with life-giving energy. First forming particles, then atoms, molecules, simple life forms, insects and plants, and then fish, birds and animals.

So, as the stream of love filled every living thing, the dream of the Circle of Love began to become real. A community of love began to grow and it continues today and into the future.

After many, many years of life evolving, people like us appeared. We human beings come from the same source as all other creatures and therefore we are all part of the same family and we depend on each other for our well-being.

Sadly we human beings don't always stay connected with the stream of love within us because we think we can make our way in life without it. As a result people focus inward and don't care for each other and other creatures.

The good news is that the stream of love keeps on flowing despite what people do, gently guiding all of life into the future.

Jesus, through the way he lived his whole life, showed people how to stay connected with the stream of love and therefore live the dream of the Circle of Love. At the centre of his life was his complete trust in the stream of love. He wanted all people to trust like he did.

Sadly again, people of Jesus' time didn't accept his way - they rejected him and had him crucified. Although alone and abandoned, he still kept trusting in the stream of love. And against all expectations he became reconnected with the wonderful expanding community of love - and he continues to be a real and on-going presence.

Looking back, we can now see that Jesus was the messenger for the Circle of Love here on Earth. He was prepared to give his life to show ordinary people that the stream of love always flows and can be depended upon, even during the most challenging times, because it will bring new life. And this applies both during and after our Earthly life.

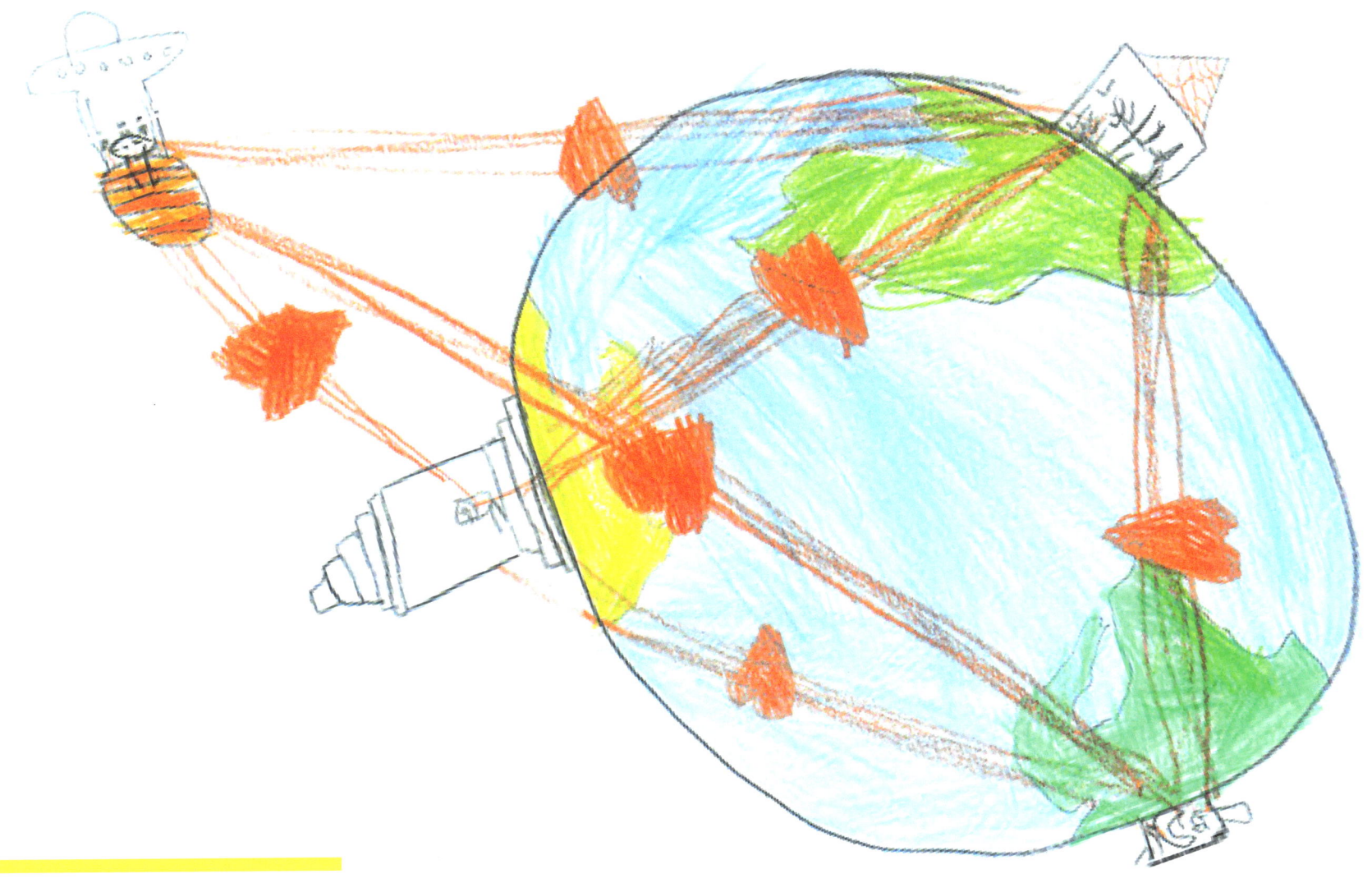

If we quieten our minds, pay attention and listen deeply, we can begin to recognise the stream of love which is actually already within us – the amazing thing is that it is there all the time! Then, inspired by Jesus, we can begin to trust it and re-connect with it.

When ordinary people connect with the stream of love and allow it to guide their lives they become one with the dream of the Circle of Love. Then regrets for past actions and fears of the future no longer hold people back. We can each be creative, seek understanding, experience wonder, care for others, work cooperatively together, and look after the Earth – this is what the dream of the Circle of Love looks like here on Earth.

As people connect with the stream of love they will grow in amazement, respect and love for every creature, every plant, and the whole biosphere, and realise that we are all part of the same wonderful expanding community of love consisting of all creatures which have ever been and ever will be.

And after our Earthly life we continue to be part of the community of love. We can offer our spiritual support to those who come after us, so they can continue the task of helping the dream become real.

In our world today people often fail to care for, or be grateful for, the wonderful creation that has evolved. Lots of healing is needed. The Circle of Love shares the pain and sorrow resulting from this failure.

Thankfully the new life which Jesus experienced after dying helps us believe that the stream of love will never stop flowing and will continue to grow the wonderful community of love – of which we will always be a part.

This is the incredible journey of the universe, and as we take our place in it, we can be confident that we will forever be cradled in the Arms of Love.

The circle of love is formed

The stream of love flows out

The community of love grows

Humans beings join the family

The stream of love keeps flowing

Human beings focus inward and are not caring

Jesus trusts in the stream of love

Jesus was rejected by the people but is still an on-going presence

Jesus is our source of hope against all the odds

The stream of love is there within us

When we connect with the stream of love the dream becomes real

The wonderful community of love continues to expand

The community of love even after our Earthly life

The dream is sometimes suppressed

Thankfully, all is cradled in the arms of love.

Ann Soo Lawrence lives in Brunswick after moving here from Sydney six years ago. Ann is married to Graham, and together with children Emma, Matthew and dog Candy, experiences great stability that supports her creative practice. Since relocating she has enjoyed exploring how art can have an impact on mental health, well-being and community building. She continues to work as a social worker in private practice and has qualifications in art therapy. This has led her to also work as a creative arts therapist with people from refugee backgrounds. Ann describes her involvement in art as an on-going journey of discovery. In collaboration with her friends at Brunswick Uniting Church through the Olive Arts Collective, she experiences love, energy and inspiration.

Richard Arnold lives in Brunswick, Victoria, Australia. He is married to Gwen and has two children Luke and Ruth who are married to Leli and James respectively, three grandsons Theo, Yosef and Thomas and a granddaughter Lucy. Richard has had a variety of careers which have exposed him to many aspects of life, including industrial chemistry, occupational health and safety, and municipal safety. Since 1999 he has been a minister in the Uniting Church in Australia. Richard currently works as a spiritual director, teaches Christian meditation and volunteers his time in various activities in his local church. Richard is a keen bird watcher and believes that our highest priorities must be conserving the environment, justly distributing the Earth's resources, and ensuring that our world moves rapidly to sustainable ways of living which protect the biosphere and all living creatures.

Thiamhien (Theo) Arnold was born on the first of January 2012 in Canberra and Yosef Arnold was born on the fifteenth of October 2013 in Melbourne. They have both lived most of their lives outside Australia including Jakarta, Indonesia and Phnom Penh, Cambodia. They have visited most countries in South East Asia as well as a number in Europe. They are both truly global citizens. They enjoy soccer, drawing, exploring new things, reading, and playing board games and chess.

www.ingramcontent.com/pod-product-compliance
Lightning Source LLC
Chambersburg PA
CBHW041325290426

44109CB00005B/129